50 Low-Calorie Snack Recipes

By: Kelly Johnson

Table of Contents

- Veggie Sticks with Hummus
- Greek Yogurt with Berries
- Air-Popped Popcorn
- Cucumber Slices with Cream Cheese
- Apple Slices with Almond Butter
- Roasted Chickpeas
- Celery with Peanut Butter
- Rice Cakes with Avocado
- Cherry Tomatoes with Feta
- Baked Sweet Potato Fries
- Carrot Sticks with Tzatziki
- Zucchini Chips
- Edamame with Sea Salt
- Cottage Cheese with Pineapple
- Hard-Boiled Eggs
- Fruit Salad with Mint
- Dark Chocolate-Dipped Strawberries
- Air-Fried Cauliflower Bites
- Sliced Bell Peppers with Salsa
- Popcorn with Nutritional Yeast
- Oven-Baked Kale Chips
- Frozen Yogurt Bark
- Homemade Trail Mix with Nuts and Dried Fruit
- Banana Slices with Cinnamon
- Jicama Sticks with Lime and Chili
- Mini Caprese Skewers
- Baked Zucchini Fries
- Cucumber and Tomato Salad
- Almonds with Dark Chocolate
- Avocado Toast on Whole Grain Bread
- Pumpkin Seeds with Spices
- Chia Seed Pudding
- Sugar Snap Peas with Ranch Dip
- Roasted Bell Pepper Strips
- Fruit and Nut Energy Balls
- Yogurt Parfait with Granola

- Baked Apple Chips
- Savory Oatmeal Cups
- Lettuce Wraps with Turkey and Veggies
- Berry Smoothie
- Pickles with Cream Cheese
- Stuffed Mini Peppers
- Cabbage Salad with Apple Cider Vinegar
- Frozen Grapes
- Spicy Avocado Dip with Veggies
- Coconut Macaroons
- Broccoli Florets with Almond Dip
- Egg Muffins with Spinach and Cheese
- Baked Pears with Cinnamon
- Sliced Strawberries with Balsamic Glaze

Veggie Sticks with Hummus

Ingredients

- 1 cup carrot sticks
- 1 cup celery sticks
- 1 cup cucumber sticks
- 1 cup bell pepper strips
- 1 cup hummus (store-bought or homemade)

Instructions

1. Arrange the veggie sticks on a platter.
2. Serve with hummus for dipping. Enjoy as a healthy snack!

Greek Yogurt with Berries

Ingredients

- 1 cup Greek yogurt (plain or flavored)
- 1/2 cup mixed berries (strawberries, blueberries, raspberries)
- 1 tablespoon honey or maple syrup (optional)
- Granola or nuts for topping (optional)

Instructions

1. In a bowl, add Greek yogurt and top with mixed berries.
2. Drizzle with honey or maple syrup if desired.
3. Sprinkle with granola or nuts for added crunch.

Air-Popped Popcorn

Ingredients

- 1/2 cup popcorn kernels
- 1 tablespoon olive oil or melted butter (optional)
- Salt to taste

Instructions

1. Pop the popcorn kernels using an air popper according to manufacturer instructions.
2. Drizzle with olive oil or melted butter if desired and sprinkle with salt. Toss to combine.

Cucumber Slices with Cream Cheese

Ingredients

- 1 cucumber, sliced into rounds
- 1/2 cup cream cheese (plain or flavored)
- Fresh herbs for garnish (optional)

Instructions

1. Spread a thin layer of cream cheese on each cucumber slice.
2. Garnish with fresh herbs if desired. Serve as a refreshing snack!

Apple Slices with Almond Butter

Ingredients

- 2 apples, sliced
- 1/4 cup almond butter

Instructions

1. Arrange apple slices on a plate.
2. Serve with almond butter for dipping.

Roasted Chickpeas

Ingredients

- 1 can (15 oz) chickpeas, drained and rinsed
- 1 tablespoon olive oil
- 1 teaspoon paprika
- 1 teaspoon garlic powder
- Salt to taste

Instructions

1. Preheat the oven to 400°F (200°C). Pat chickpeas dry with a paper towel.
2. In a bowl, toss chickpeas with olive oil, paprika, garlic powder, and salt.
3. Spread on a baking sheet and roast for 20-25 minutes, stirring occasionally, until crispy.

Celery with Peanut Butter

Ingredients

- 4 celery stalks, cut into sticks
- 1/4 cup peanut butter

Instructions

1. Fill the celery sticks with peanut butter.
2. Enjoy as a crunchy and satisfying snack!

Rice Cakes with Avocado

Ingredients

- 4 rice cakes
- 1 avocado, mashed
- Salt and pepper to taste
- Optional toppings: cherry tomatoes, red pepper flakes, or lemon juice

Instructions

1. Spread mashed avocado evenly on each rice cake.
2. Season with salt and pepper. Add optional toppings if desired. Enjoy!

Cherry Tomatoes with Feta

Ingredients

- 2 cups cherry tomatoes, halved
- 1/2 cup feta cheese, crumbled
- 2 tablespoons olive oil
- Fresh basil or parsley for garnish
- Salt and pepper to taste

Instructions

1. In a bowl, combine cherry tomatoes and feta cheese.
2. Drizzle with olive oil and season with salt and pepper. Toss gently.
3. Garnish with fresh herbs and serve.

Baked Sweet Potato Fries

Ingredients

- 2 large sweet potatoes, cut into fries
- 2 tablespoons olive oil
- 1 teaspoon paprika
- 1/2 teaspoon garlic powder
- Salt and pepper to taste

Instructions

1. Preheat the oven to 425°F (220°C).
2. Toss sweet potato fries with olive oil, paprika, garlic powder, salt, and pepper.
3. Spread on a baking sheet in a single layer and bake for 25-30 minutes, flipping halfway through, until crispy.

Carrot Sticks with Tzatziki

Ingredients

- 4 large carrots, cut into sticks
- 1 cup tzatziki sauce (store-bought or homemade)

Instructions

1. Arrange carrot sticks on a platter.
2. Serve with tzatziki sauce for dipping.

Zucchini Chips

Ingredients

- 2 medium zucchinis, thinly sliced
- 2 tablespoons olive oil
- Salt and pepper to taste
- Optional: garlic powder or Italian seasoning

Instructions

1. Preheat the oven to 225°F (110°C).
2. Toss zucchini slices with olive oil, salt, pepper, and any optional seasonings.
3. Spread on a baking sheet in a single layer and bake for 1-2 hours until crisp, flipping halfway through.

Edamame with Sea Salt

Ingredients

- 2 cups edamame (in pods)
- Sea salt to taste

Instructions

1. Boil edamame in salted water for about 5 minutes until tender.
2. Drain and sprinkle with sea salt. Serve warm or at room temperature.

Cottage Cheese with Pineapple

Ingredients

- 1 cup cottage cheese
- 1/2 cup pineapple chunks (fresh or canned)

Instructions

1. In a bowl, combine cottage cheese and pineapple chunks.
2. Stir gently and enjoy as a protein-packed snack.

Hard-Boiled Eggs

Ingredients

- 4 eggs
- Salt and pepper to taste

Instructions

1. Place eggs in a pot and cover with water. Bring to a boil over medium heat.
2. Once boiling, cover and remove from heat. Let sit for 12-15 minutes.
3. Transfer eggs to an ice bath, then peel and season with salt and pepper.

Fruit Salad with Mint

Ingredients

- 2 cups mixed fresh fruit (e.g., berries, melon, kiwi, apple)
- 2 tablespoons fresh mint leaves, chopped
- 1 tablespoon honey or lime juice (optional)

Instructions

1. In a bowl, combine mixed fresh fruit and chopped mint.
2. Drizzle with honey or lime juice if desired. Toss gently and serve chilled.

Dark Chocolate-Dipped Strawberries

Ingredients

- 1 pound fresh strawberries, washed and dried
- 8 ounces dark chocolate, chopped
- Optional toppings: crushed nuts, sprinkles, or sea salt

Instructions

1. Melt the dark chocolate in a microwave-safe bowl in 30-second intervals, stirring until smooth.
2. Dip each strawberry into the melted chocolate, allowing excess to drip off.
3. Place dipped strawberries on a parchment-lined baking sheet and add any optional toppings. Refrigerate until set.

Air-Fried Cauliflower Bites

Ingredients

- 1 medium head of cauliflower, cut into florets
- 2 tablespoons olive oil
- 1 teaspoon garlic powder
- 1 teaspoon paprika
- Salt and pepper to taste

Instructions

1. Preheat the air fryer to 400°F (200°C).
2. Toss cauliflower florets with olive oil, garlic powder, paprika, salt, and pepper.
3. Place in the air fryer basket and cook for 10-12 minutes, shaking halfway through, until golden and tender.

Sliced Bell Peppers with Salsa

Ingredients

- 2-3 assorted bell peppers, sliced
- 1 cup salsa (store-bought or homemade)

Instructions

1. Arrange sliced bell peppers on a platter.
2. Serve with salsa for dipping.

Popcorn with Nutritional Yeast

Ingredients

- 1/2 cup popcorn kernels (or pre-popped popcorn)
- 2 tablespoons nutritional yeast
- 1 tablespoon olive oil (optional)
- Salt to taste

Instructions

1. Pop the popcorn using an air popper or stovetop method.
2. In a large bowl, drizzle with olive oil (if using) and sprinkle with nutritional yeast and salt. Toss to coat evenly.

Oven-Baked Kale Chips

Ingredients

- 1 bunch kale, washed and dried
- 1 tablespoon olive oil
- Salt to taste

Instructions

1. Preheat the oven to 300°F (150°C).
2. Tear kale leaves into bite-sized pieces and toss with olive oil and salt.
3. Spread on a baking sheet in a single layer and bake for 15-20 minutes, until crisp and lightly browned.

Frozen Yogurt Bark

Ingredients

- 2 cups Greek yogurt (any flavor)
- 1/2 cup mixed berries (fresh or frozen)
- 1/4 cup nuts or granola (optional)

Instructions

1. Spread yogurt evenly on a parchment-lined baking sheet.
2. Top with mixed berries and nuts or granola, pressing them into the yogurt.
3. Freeze for at least 2 hours, then break into pieces and serve.

Homemade Trail Mix with Nuts and Dried Fruit

Ingredients

- 1 cup mixed nuts (e.g., almonds, walnuts, cashews)
- 1 cup dried fruit (e.g., cranberries, raisins, apricots)
- Optional: dark chocolate chips or seeds

Instructions

1. In a large bowl, combine mixed nuts, dried fruit, and any optional ingredients.
2. Store in an airtight container for a quick and healthy snack.

Banana Slices with Cinnamon

Ingredients

- 2 bananas, sliced
- Ground cinnamon to taste

Instructions

1. Arrange banana slices on a plate.
2. Sprinkle with ground cinnamon and enjoy as a simple snack.

Jicama Sticks with Lime and Chili

Ingredients

- 1 medium jicama, peeled and cut into sticks
- Juice of 1 lime
- 1 teaspoon chili powder
- Salt to taste

Instructions

1. In a large bowl, toss jicama sticks with lime juice, chili powder, and salt until evenly coated.
2. Serve chilled as a refreshing snack.

Mini Caprese Skewers

Ingredients

- 1 pint cherry tomatoes
- 8 ounces fresh mozzarella balls (bocconcini)
- Fresh basil leaves
- Balsamic glaze (for drizzling)
- Salt and pepper to taste

Instructions

1. Thread a cherry tomato, a basil leaf, and a mozzarella ball onto toothpicks or small skewers.
2. Drizzle with balsamic glaze and sprinkle with salt and pepper before serving.

Baked Zucchini Fries

Ingredients

- 2 medium zucchinis, cut into sticks
- 1 cup breadcrumbs (or panko)
- 1/2 cup grated Parmesan cheese
- 1 teaspoon garlic powder
- 2 eggs, beaten
- Salt and pepper to taste

Instructions

1. Preheat the oven to 425°F (220°C) and line a baking sheet with parchment paper.
2. In a bowl, mix breadcrumbs, Parmesan, garlic powder, salt, and pepper.
3. Dip zucchini sticks in beaten eggs, then coat with the breadcrumb mixture. Place on the prepared baking sheet.
4. Bake for 20-25 minutes, until golden and crispy.

Cucumber and Tomato Salad

Ingredients

- 2 cups cherry tomatoes, halved
- 1 large cucumber, diced
- 1/4 red onion, thinly sliced
- 2 tablespoons olive oil
- 1 tablespoon red wine vinegar
- Salt and pepper to taste

Instructions

1. In a large bowl, combine cherry tomatoes, cucumber, and red onion.
2. Drizzle with olive oil and red wine vinegar. Season with salt and pepper, then toss to combine.

Almonds with Dark Chocolate

Ingredients

- 1 cup raw almonds
- 1 cup dark chocolate chips (or chopped dark chocolate)

Instructions

1. Melt dark chocolate in a microwave-safe bowl in 30-second intervals, stirring until smooth.
2. Add almonds to the melted chocolate, mixing until coated.
3. Spread the chocolate-covered almonds on a parchment-lined baking sheet and let cool until set.

Avocado Toast on Whole Grain Bread

Ingredients

- 2 slices whole grain bread, toasted
- 1 ripe avocado
- Juice of 1/2 lime
- Salt and pepper to taste
- Optional toppings: cherry tomatoes, radishes, feta cheese, or red pepper flakes

Instructions

1. In a bowl, mash the avocado with lime juice, salt, and pepper.
2. Spread the mashed avocado evenly over the toasted bread.
3. Top with any optional toppings before serving.

Pumpkin Seeds with Spices

Ingredients

- 1 cup raw pumpkin seeds (pepitas)
- 1 tablespoon olive oil
- 1 teaspoon smoked paprika
- 1/2 teaspoon garlic powder
- Salt to taste

Instructions

1. Preheat the oven to 350°F (175°C) and line a baking sheet with parchment paper.
2. In a bowl, mix pumpkin seeds with olive oil, smoked paprika, garlic powder, and salt until well coated.
3. Spread in a single layer on the baking sheet and bake for 10-15 minutes, stirring occasionally, until toasted.

Chia Seed Pudding

Ingredients

- 1/2 cup chia seeds
- 2 cups almond milk (or any milk of choice)
- 2 tablespoons maple syrup or honey
- 1 teaspoon vanilla extract
- Optional toppings: fresh fruit, nuts, or granola

Instructions

1. In a bowl, whisk together chia seeds, almond milk, maple syrup, and vanilla extract until combined.
2. Let sit for 5 minutes, then whisk again to prevent clumping.
3. Cover and refrigerate for at least 2 hours or overnight until thickened. Serve with desired toppings.

Sugar Snap Peas with Ranch Dip

Ingredients

- 2 cups sugar snap peas, trimmed
- 1/2 cup ranch dressing (store-bought or homemade)

Instructions

1. Serve sugar snap peas raw with ranch dressing for dipping. Enjoy as a crunchy, refreshing snack.

Roasted Bell Pepper Strips

Ingredients

- 2 bell peppers (any color), sliced into strips
- 2 tablespoons olive oil
- Salt and pepper to taste
- Optional: garlic powder, Italian seasoning

Instructions

1. Preheat the oven to 425°F (220°C).
2. Toss bell pepper strips with olive oil, salt, pepper, and any optional seasonings.
3. Spread the peppers on a baking sheet and roast for 20-25 minutes until tender and slightly charred.

Fruit and Nut Energy Balls

Ingredients

- 1 cup dates, pitted
- 1 cup nuts (almonds, walnuts, or pecans)
- 1/2 cup rolled oats
- 1/4 cup nut butter (peanut, almond, or cashew)
- 1/2 teaspoon vanilla extract

Instructions

1. In a food processor, combine dates, nuts, oats, nut butter, and vanilla extract.
2. Blend until a sticky dough forms. If too dry, add a little water or more nut butter.
3. Roll into small balls and refrigerate until firm.

Yogurt Parfait with Granola

Ingredients

- 2 cups Greek yogurt (or regular yogurt)
- 1 cup granola
- 1 cup mixed berries (strawberries, blueberries, raspberries)
- Honey or maple syrup (optional)

Instructions

1. In a glass or bowl, layer Greek yogurt, granola, and mixed berries.
2. Drizzle with honey or maple syrup if desired. Repeat layers until all ingredients are used.

Baked Apple Chips

Ingredients

- 2-3 apples, thinly sliced
- 1 teaspoon cinnamon
- Optional: sugar or sweetener to taste

Instructions

1. Preheat the oven to 225°F (110°C) and line a baking sheet with parchment paper.
2. Arrange apple slices in a single layer on the baking sheet. Sprinkle with cinnamon and optional sugar.
3. Bake for 1-2 hours until dry and crisp, flipping halfway through.

Savory Oatmeal Cups

Ingredients

- 2 cups rolled oats
- 2 cups vegetable or chicken broth
- 1 cup chopped vegetables (spinach, bell peppers, onions)
- 1/2 cup shredded cheese (cheddar or mozzarella)
- 2 eggs
- Salt and pepper to taste

Instructions

1. Preheat the oven to 350°F (175°C) and grease a muffin tin.
2. In a large bowl, mix oats, broth, chopped vegetables, cheese, eggs, salt, and pepper.
3. Spoon the mixture into the muffin tin, filling each cup about 3/4 full. Bake for 20-25 minutes until set and golden.

Lettuce Wraps with Turkey and Veggies

Ingredients

- 1 pound ground turkey
- 1 tablespoon soy sauce
- 1 teaspoon sesame oil
- 1 cup diced vegetables (carrots, bell peppers, green onions)
- Lettuce leaves (butter lettuce or romaine)
- Optional toppings: chopped cilantro, chopped peanuts, sriracha

Instructions

1. In a skillet, cook ground turkey over medium heat until browned. Add soy sauce, sesame oil, and diced vegetables. Cook until vegetables are tender.
2. Spoon the turkey mixture onto lettuce leaves and top with optional toppings before serving.

Berry Smoothie

Ingredients

- 1 cup mixed berries (fresh or frozen)
- 1 banana
- 1 cup almond milk (or any milk of choice)
- 1 tablespoon honey or maple syrup (optional)
- Optional: 1 tablespoon chia seeds or protein powder

Instructions

1. In a blender, combine mixed berries, banana, almond milk, honey (if using), and any optional ingredients.
2. Blend until smooth and creamy. Pour into a glass and enjoy!

Pickles with Cream Cheese

Ingredients

- 12-15 dill pickles (whole or sliced)
- 8 ounces cream cheese, softened
- Optional: fresh herbs (dill or chives) for garnish

Instructions

1. If using whole pickles, slice them in half lengthwise. If using slices, leave them as is.
2. Spread a generous layer of cream cheese onto each pickle slice or half.
3. Garnish with fresh herbs if desired. Serve immediately or refrigerate until ready to serve.

Stuffed Mini Peppers

Ingredients

- 12 mini sweet peppers, halved and seeded
- 8 ounces cream cheese, softened
- 1/2 cup shredded cheese (cheddar or mozzarella)
- 1/4 cup diced green onions or chives
- Salt and pepper to taste

Instructions

1. Preheat the oven to 375°F (190°C).
2. In a mixing bowl, combine cream cheese, shredded cheese, green onions, salt, and pepper.
3. Stuff each mini pepper half with the cheese mixture and place on a baking sheet.
4. Bake for 15-20 minutes until the cheese is bubbly and the peppers are tender.

Cabbage Salad with Apple Cider Vinegar

Ingredients

- 4 cups shredded cabbage (green or purple)
- 1 cup shredded carrots
- 1/2 cup diced bell pepper
- 1/4 cup apple cider vinegar
- 2 tablespoons olive oil
- Salt and pepper to taste

Instructions

1. In a large bowl, combine shredded cabbage, carrots, and bell pepper.
2. In a separate bowl, whisk together apple cider vinegar, olive oil, salt, and pepper.
3. Pour the dressing over the salad and toss to coat. Let sit for 15 minutes before serving to allow the flavors to meld.

Frozen Grapes

Ingredients

- 2 cups seedless grapes (red or green)

Instructions

1. Rinse the grapes under cold water and remove any stems.
2. Pat dry and spread them out on a baking sheet in a single layer.
3. Freeze for at least 2 hours until solid. Serve as a refreshing snack.

Spicy Avocado Dip with Veggies

Ingredients

- 2 ripe avocados
- 1 tablespoon lime juice
- 1 teaspoon chili powder (or to taste)
- Salt to taste
- Veggies for dipping (carrot sticks, cucumber slices, bell pepper strips)

Instructions

1. In a bowl, mash the avocados and mix in lime juice, chili powder, and salt until smooth.
2. Serve the spicy avocado dip with assorted veggies for dipping. Enjoy!

Coconut Macaroons

Ingredients

- 3 cups shredded unsweetened coconut
- 1/2 cup granulated sugar
- 1/4 cup all-purpose flour
- 1/4 teaspoon salt
- 4 large egg whites
- 1 teaspoon vanilla extract
- Optional: melted chocolate for drizzling

Instructions

1. Preheat the oven to 325°F (160°C) and line a baking sheet with parchment paper.
2. In a large bowl, mix the shredded coconut, sugar, flour, and salt.
3. In a separate bowl, beat the egg whites and vanilla until soft peaks form.
4. Gently fold the egg whites into the coconut mixture until combined.
5. Using a tablespoon or cookie scoop, drop the mixture onto the prepared baking sheet.
6. Bake for 20-25 minutes, or until golden brown. Allow to cool completely.
7. If desired, drizzle with melted chocolate before serving.

Broccoli Florets with Almond Dip

Ingredients

- 2 cups fresh broccoli florets
- 1/2 cup almond butter
- 1 tablespoon soy sauce
- 1 tablespoon maple syrup or honey
- 1 tablespoon lemon juice
- Water to thin (as needed)

Instructions

1. In a small bowl, whisk together almond butter, soy sauce, maple syrup, lemon juice, and enough water to achieve desired dip consistency.
2. Steam or blanch broccoli florets until bright green and tender-crisp, about 2-3 minutes.
3. Serve the broccoli florets with the almond dip on the side.

Egg Muffins with Spinach and Cheese

Ingredients

- 6 large eggs
- 1 cup fresh spinach, chopped
- 1/2 cup shredded cheese (cheddar, feta, or your choice)
- Salt and pepper to taste
- Optional: diced bell peppers or onions

Instructions

1. Preheat the oven to 350°F (175°C) and grease a muffin tin.
2. In a mixing bowl, whisk together the eggs, salt, and pepper.
3. Stir in the chopped spinach, cheese, and any additional vegetables.
4. Pour the egg mixture evenly into the muffin tin, filling each cup about 3/4 full.
5. Bake for 20-25 minutes, or until the egg muffins are set and slightly golden. Allow to cool before removing from the tin.

Baked Pears with Cinnamon

Ingredients

- 2 ripe pears, halved and cored
- 2 tablespoons brown sugar
- 1 teaspoon cinnamon
- Optional: chopped nuts for topping

Instructions

1. Preheat the oven to 350°F (175°C) and line a baking dish with parchment paper.
2. Place the pear halves cut side up in the baking dish.
3. Sprinkle brown sugar and cinnamon over the pears.
4. Bake for 20-25 minutes, until tender and caramelized. Top with chopped nuts if desired.

Sliced Strawberries with Balsamic Glaze

Ingredients

- 2 cups fresh strawberries, hulled and sliced
- 2 tablespoons balsamic glaze (store-bought or homemade)
- Optional: fresh mint for garnish

Instructions

1. Place sliced strawberries in a bowl.
2. Drizzle with balsamic glaze and gently toss to coat.
3. Serve immediately, garnished with fresh mint if desired.

www.ingramcontent.com/pod-product-compliance
Lightning Source LLC
LaVergne TN
LVHW061955070526
838199LV00060B/4138